Islam: An Introduction

(Selected Writings)

Ahsan Academy of Research
(Springs, South Africa)

Islam: An Introduction
(Selected Writings)

by
Fazlur Rahman Ansari

Edited by
Abdul Kader Choughley

Tawasul International
Centre for Publishing, Research and Dialogue

First Published 2024

ISBN : 979-12-81473-386

Edited by Abdul Kader Choughley

Ahsan Academy of Research
(Springs, South Africa)
ahsan@worldonline.co.za

SHELVCRAFT™
Shelving | Racking | Display | Shop Fitting Ph:
012 666 8933
Email: sales@shelvcraft.com
Website: www.shelvcraft.com

Published by
Tawasul International
Centre for Publishing, Research and Dialogue, Rome, Italy

CONTENTS

Preface.. 7

Chapter I: A Fundamental View of Islam 9

Chapter II: Islam: A Guide... 19

Chapter III: Philosophy of Worship ('Ibādah) in Islam 44

Preface

The present work comprises three booklets written by Mawlānā Dr. Fazlur Rahman Ansari in the early years of his academic career. As a *muballigh*, Ansari's articles provided a rational exposition about the beliefs and tenets of Islam. It must be noted that the articles were written in a historical context. The influence of *orientalism*, under the patronage of British colonialism, posed a major challenge to Islam. Under the guise of academic scholarship, Western writers attempted to malign Islamic teachings and the Holy Prophet (pbuh). It was in response to these fabricated versions of Islam that Ansari's articles made appropriate references to Western critics, who in several instances, grudgingly accepted Islam's impact as a global civilisation. Ansari's broad knowledge of modern science and his erudite Islamic learning enabled him to contextualise the relevance of Islam and its message to a contemporary audience. Unlike Muslim modernists who emerged as the apologetic face of Islam, Ansari vigorously presented the holistic dimensions of Islam based on their perennial sources, the Qur'ān and Sunnah.

The first article, *A Fundamental View of Islam* examines, albeit briefly, key concepts that have a direct bearing on the integral role of unity (*tawhid*). The Qur'ān states unambiguously that *tawhid* permeates every facet of human endeavour; therefore, the dualistic vision embraced by other world religions and subsequently advanced by Western civilisation defeats the integrated philosophy of Islam.

A synopsis of Islamic faith and practice is presented in *Islam: A Guide*. The salient features are supported by an array of opinions and impressions from the writings of Western critics of Islam. Ansari's reference to Western sources does in no way betray an apologetic mindset. On the contrary, he is able to convincingly articulate the significance of Islamic teachings which over the centuries have guided Muslim collective life. The enduring legacy of Islam, according to Ansari, continues to open up new pathways of understanding the universal message of the Qur'ān.

As title of the article suggests, *Philosophy of Worship in Islam* has a broader connotation. Ansari elucidates the rationale behind the pillars of Islam (*arkān*) and also outlines the wisdom that informs the Prophetic practices in this regard. His significant contributions serve as an unbroken link to previous scholarly studies on Islamic faith and practice. As a dynamic scholar, Ansari's profound study of the Qur'ān and tafsir literature equipped him to restate Islamic teachings in a contemporary setting. The thematic significance of these articles is aimed at rediscovering the message of Islam to the modern mind.

The articles in the present work have been edited to provide fluency to the text. The translation of Qur'ānic verses (*āyāt*) are in many instances paraphrased by Ansari and do not necessarily convey a literal or idiomatic meaning.

Anver Essa deserves special mention for his unfailing support in promoting the works of Mawlānā Ansari.

Abdul Kader Choughley
Springs (South Africa)
30 November 2019

Chapter I

A Fundamental View of Islam

What is the character of the universe which we inhabit, and how are we related to it? These are the two fundamental questions which have confronted all religions and philosophies of the world, and each religious and philosophical system has tried to answer them in its own way.

Closely connected with these questions is the problem of the nature of relationship between mind and matter – between the spiritual and physical aspects of life, and a solution of this problem alone can form the basis of our worldview and our life-programme.

There are three distinct answers offered to our inquiry in this connection, through the pre-Islamic religions, the post-Islamic empirical thought of the West, and Islam.

Pre-Islamic Religions

The pre-Islamic religions were deeply impressed by the notion of an acute conflict between man's moral and physical existence, or in other words, between 'the biological within' and 'the mathematical without'. This dualistic idea led them ultimately to find a way for the affirmation of the spiritual self in man in the rejection of the physical reality as either meaningless or dangerous. Hinduism regarded the world of matter as *maya*, an illusion, and prescribed a life of renunciation for the spiritual development of its devotees. Buddhism considered the physical world an obstruction in the onward march of the soul, and pointed to the annihilation of the individual self and the severance of its emotional links with the material world as the way to achieve *nirvana*. Christianity similarly endorsed the antagonism between the physical and spiritual aspects of life and conceived the world of matter, or to use a more Christian term, the world of the flesh, as essentially the playground of Satan. Consequently, it standardised perfection in the type of the ascetic saint[1].

Such a despising attitude towards the material aspect of life affects humanity in two ways. Firstly, it shuts the door to all material progress, not to speak of scientific advancement, because our involvement in material pursuits is considered detrimental to the ideal of spiritual self-realisation. Secondly, it gives rise to a perpetual conflict within us, because on the one side, is the religious call to shun the world, while on the other side, exists the natural urge to enjoy it. Such a state of affairs can only culminate in creating a continuous feeling of bad conscience and thus defeating the very purpose of our idealistic attitude.

Post-Islamic Empirical Thought of the West

The post-Islamic empirical thought of the West adopts a path which is radically different from the pre-Islamic idealism. It asserts that the world of matter alone is real and worthy of our attention and that the realisation of human destiny lies in the conquest of nature with the ultimate aim of achieving the highest form of physical pleasure. It ignores all transcendental values and spiritual considerations simply because they do not fall within the scope of empirical sciences. Hence, there is only one criterion of practical utility for the enhancement of the earthly or 'carnal' pleasures of man.

Now, the physical world being essentially a battlefield of conflicting appearances, an exclusively materialistic interpretation of reality, even though it may be concealed behind the otherwise fascinating mask of scientific spirit, is bound to unbalance human life.[2] This is what the West is experiencing today. Nations are

---

[1] For a detailed exposition on the religious outlook of these religions, see Fazlur Rahman Ansari, *The Qur'ānic Foundations and Structure of Muslim Society*, vol. 1 (Karachi, Dar-ul- Ishaat, 1994), 104-112.

[2] Ansari's critique of Western civilisation focuses on its materialistic philosophy. It has spawned secularism which negates the primary importance of *wahy* (revelation) as the bedrock of human guidance. See Mahdie Kriel, *Islamic Intellectual Revival of the Modern Mind* (Cape Town, Iqra Publishers, 2011), 5-6.

running at the throats of each other and individuals are indulging in the pleasures of the flesh in a way which preclude all possibilities of life's spiritual expression. Peace and piety both have been thrown away to the winds.

Islam

What then is the message of Islam which stands between the ancient world which stressed the exclusive validity of the spiritual aspect of life, and the modern world which interprets all reality in terms of matter? Has it any solution to offer to reconcile this sharp antagonism? Has it any teachings to give in the light of which we may develop all our faculties evenly and work out our destiny without prejudice against either our natural surroundings and the physical conditions of our life or our idealistic yearnings?

To start with: Islam does not consider the universe as composed of two self-existing and conflicting entities. It conceives all life as a unity because it proceeds from the Divine Oneness (*tawhid*). Thus the real world is a coherent organic unity, spaceless and timeless, but which includes all happenings in space and time in their proper relations to itself.

In addition to this principle of harmony, Islam emphasises the purpose and nature of all existence, whether spiritual or physical. Allah says in the Qur'ān:

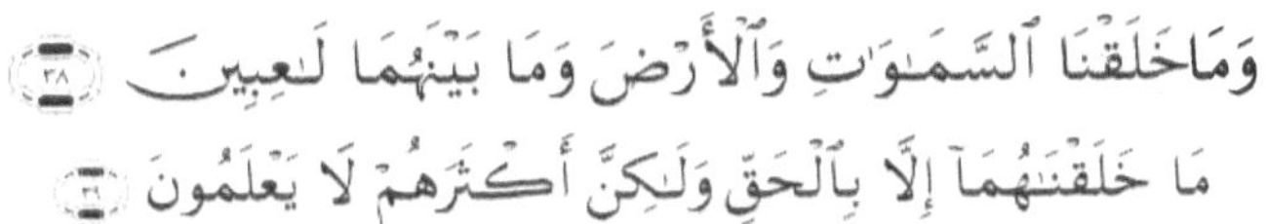

"We have not created the heavens and the earth and whatever is between them in sport. We have not created them but for a serious end; but the greater part of them understand not."[3]

Thus our earthly surroundings are not a meaningless projection of the play of blind forces - a mere empty shell with not content.

---

[3] al-Dukhān: 38-9.

Nay, the tiniest particle of sand, the smallest drop of water, the frailest rose-leaf are full of meaning and music and function under a definite and well-planned Divine scheme.

Man: Vicegerent of Allah

This being the character of the universe, what is the nature of man? Should we conceive him as a being who is originally born low and who cannot attain the pinnacle of purity and perfection except through the tragedy of renouncing the worldly pleasure or of passing through a continuous ordeal of transmigration? This is the way Hinduism, Buddhism and some other religions go. Or, should we believe him to have been born in sin and therefore incapable of working out his destiny except through a mysterious divine sacrifice? This is the doctrine of Christianity. To these questions, Islam replies in the negative. It is emphatic in its assertion that man is born sinless and is the chosen of Allah, as we read in the following verses (*āyāt*):

$$\text{لَقَدْ خَلَقْنَا ٱلْإِنسَـٰنَ فِى أَحْسَنِ تَقْوِيمٍ}$$

"Of the goodliest fibre we created man"[4]

$$\text{وَهُوَ ٱلَّذِى جَعَلَكُمْ خَلَـٰٓئِفَ ٱلْأَرْضِ}$$

"And it is He who hath made you His vicegerents on the earth..."[5]

Starting his life with a sinless birth, man is entitled, or we might say, destined, as an evolutionary being to scale the loftiest heights of perfection and to surpass all the creation of Allah including the angels, in his uniqueness and purity.

---

[4] al-Tin: 4.
[5] al-An‘ām: 165.

Principle of Unity

What then should be our attitude towards our material environment? Should it consist in renouncing the world and repressing our physical desires? Islam says nothing of the kind. Instead of recognising a conflict between the moral and physical existence of man, it highlights the co-existence of these two aspects as the natural basis of life. It maintains that our earthly sojourn is an integral factor in the Divine scheme of creation and a necessary stage in the evolution of our soul-life. Consequently, it seeks the affirmation of the spiritual self in man, not in renouncing the world of matter, but in the active endeavour to master it with a view to discover a basis for a realistic regulation of life. It is therefore impossible for Islam to despise our earthly existence and activities, and here it differs radically with other religions of the world.

This realistic attitude of Islam may not however be identified with that of the modern West. The latter ignores our spiritual existence altogether and regards our earthly career as an end-in-itself, and that in a way is equated to worship of materialism. Islam, on the other hand, conceives it not as the end but as a means to a higher spiritual end.

And what is that higher end? It is submission to the will of Allah and seeking His pleasure, as the Qur'ān says:

$$\text{قُلْ إِنَّ صَلَاتِي وَنُسُكِي وَمَحْيَايَ وَمَمَاتِي لِلَّهِ رَبِّ ٱلْعَالَمِينَ}$$

"Say: Verily, my worship and my sacrifice and my living and my dying are for Allah, Lord of the Worlds."[6]

Islamic Concept of Worship

Viewed in this light, all our worldly actions, including the most insignificant ones, are transformed into religious acts (*'ibādah*), the

---

[6] al-An'ām: 162.

moment we give them a spiritual orientation. We perform *'ibādah* with the consciousness that we are acting in the light of Allah's commands. In fact, Islam envisages the whole life of a Muslim as a life of continuous worship. Allah says in the Qur'ān:

$$\text{وَمَا خَلَقْتُ ٱلْجِنَّ وَٱلْإِنسَ إِلَّا لِيَعْبُدُونِ ٥٦}$$

"I have not created the Jinn and humankind but that they shall worship Me."[7]

Thus the notion of worship in Islam is also radically different from that of other religions. In Islam there is no such distinction as 'religious' and 'secular'. Every act of a true Muslim is a religious act because he has to perform all his works in obedience and conformity to Divine injunctions and has to dedicate all his faculties, spiritual or physical, to the cause of Allah's eternal scheme. Devotion and submission to Allah in this sense constitute the very meaning of our life in Islam.

This being the case, it was absolutely necessary that Islam should not confine itself to the explanation of the metaphysical relations between man and his Creator but should also define exactly the relationship between the individual and society. Thus Islam has given us an exhaustive guidance which does not leave even the most trivial actions of our life untouched.

Principle of Movement

The essential nature of the Islamic view of life must have become clear from what has been said above. But it is mostly the principle of 'unity of life' that has been elaborated so far. There is, however, another fundamental principle also, namely, 'movement in life', which needs some elucidation. In this connection, the discussion might be confined to an examination of Islam's attitude towards the empirical sciences, which, is, however, the direct

---

[7] al-Dhāriyāt: 56.

outcome of its realistic conception of nature and man.

The Holy Prophet (pbuh) stands alone in the religious annals of the world as the advocate of scientific inquiry. The pages of the Qur'ān abound with passages which invite our attention to an empirical study of the natural phenomena and the conquest of nature by man. In fact, the inductive method of inquiry,[8] which is the basis of modern scientific and philosophical thought, is one of the most valuable gifts of the Qur'ān to the world. Let me cite here just a few Qur'ānic verses (āyāt) to substantiate this statement. The Qur'ān says:

إِنَّ فِى خَلْقِ ٱلسَّمَـٰوَٰتِ وَٱلْأَرْضِ وَٱخْتِلَـٰفِ ٱلَّيْلِ وَٱلنَّهَارِ وَٱلْفُلْكِ ٱلَّتِى تَجْرِى فِى ٱلْبَحْرِ بِمَا يَنفَعُ ٱلنَّاسَ وَمَآ أَنزَلَ ٱللَّهُ مِنَ ٱلسَّمَآءِ مِن مَّآءٍ فَأَحْيَا بِهِ ٱلْأَرْضَ بَعْدَ مَوْتِهَا وَبَثَّ فِيهَا مِن كُلِّ دَآبَّةٍ وَتَصْرِيفِ ٱلرِّيَـٰحِ وَٱلسَّحَابِ ٱلْمُسَخَّرِ بَيْنَ ٱلسَّمَآءِ وَٱلْأَرْضِ لَآيَـٰتٍ لِّقَوْمٍ يَعْقِلُونَ ۝

"Assuredly, in the creation of the heavens and of the earth, and in the alternation of night and day; and in the ships which pass through the sea with what is useful to man; and in the rain which Allah sends down from heaven, giving life to the earth after its death, and scattering over it all kinds of animals; and in the change of winds; and in the clouds that are made to do service between the heavens and the earth -are signs for those who understand."[9]

---

[8] The inductive method of enquiry inaugurated by Islam has been lucidly explained in Ansari's article: *The Holy Prophet's (SAW) Contribution to Knowledge*, in The Minaret, 14:5 May 1975. Cf. Abul Hasan Ali Nadwi, *Islam and Knowledge* (Oxford OCIS, 1988).
[9] al-Baqarah: 164.

وَمِنْ ءَايَتِهِۦ خَلْقُ ٱلسَّمَـٰوَٰتِ وَٱلْأَرْضِ وَٱخْتِلَـٰفُ أَلْسِنَتِكُمْ وَأَلْوَٰنِكُمْ إِنَّ فِى ذَٰلِكَ لَـٔايَـٰتٍ لِّلْعَـٰلِمِينَ ﴿٢٢﴾

"And among His signs are the creation of the heavens and of the earth, and your variety of tongues and colours. Herein truly are signs for men of knowledge."[10]

It is no wonder, therefore, that during the age of Islam's glory, its followers became the pioneers of civilisation and the inaugurators of the modern scientific era. It might sound strange to those who are accustomed to hear that Islam obstructs the way to progress and is an enemy of scientific learning, and that the Muslims are a race of barbarians. The truth lies just the opposite way, and it can honestly be said that but for Islam there would have been no modern scientific civilisation. Let me quote Robert Briffault, a great non-Muslim authority of the West. He says in his reputed work, *The Making of Humanity:*

Neither Roger Bacon nor his later name- sake has any title to be credited with having introduced the experimental method. Roger Bacon was no more than one of the apostles of Muslim science and method to Christian Europe. Science is the momentous contribution of Arab civilisation to the modern world, (though) it was not science only which brought Europe back to life. Other and manifold influences from the civilisation of Islam communicated it first glow to European life.[11]

The debt of our science to that of the Arabs does not consist in startling discoveries of revolutionary theories; science owes a great deal more to Arab culture; it owes its existence. The ancient world was, as we saw, pre-scientific. The Astronomy and Mathematics of the Greeks were a foreign importation never thoroughly acclimatised in Greek culture. The Greeks systematised, generalised and theorised, but the patient ways of

---

[10] al-Rum: 22.
[11] Robert Briffault, *The Making of Humanity* (London, 1919), 202.

investigation, the accumulation of positive knowledge, the minute methods of science, detailed and prolonged observation and experimental inquiry were altogether alien to Greek temperament. What we call science arose in Europe as a result of a new spirit of inquiry, of new methods of investigation, of the method of experiment, observation, measurement, of the development of Mathematics in a form unknown to the Greeks. That spirit and those methods were introduced into the European world by the Arabs.[12]

A vital point of difference between the spirit of modern West and the spirit of Islam may however be stated again. While the modern West has employed science mostly for the satisfaction of its craving after power and pleasure, Islam seeks in the scientific inquiry a means to the service of humanity and spiritual elevation. How beautifully has the Qur'ān inculcated the latter idea in the following verse (*āyah*):

إِنَّ فِي خَلْقِ ٱلسَّمَـٰوَٰتِ وَٱلْأَرْضِ وَٱخْتِلَـٰفِ ٱلَّيْلِ وَٱلنَّهَارِ لَأَيَـٰتٍ

لِّأُوْلِى ٱلْأَلْبَـٰبِ ٱلَّذِينَ يَذْكُرُونَ ٱللَّهَ قِيَـٰمًا وَقُعُودًا وَعَلَىٰ جُنُوبِهِمْ

وَيَتَفَكَّرُونَ فِي خَلْقِ ٱلسَّمَـٰوَٰتِ وَٱلْأَرْضِ رَبَّنَا مَا خَلَقْتَ هَـٰذَا بَـٰطِلًا

سُبْحَـٰنَكَ فَقِنَا عَذَابَ ٱلنَّارِ ۝

"Verily in the creation of the heavens and of the earth, and in the succession of night and day, are signs for men of understanding. Who, standing and sitting and reclining, bear Allah in mind and reflect on the creation of the heavens and of the earth, and say: Oh, our Lord! Thou has not created all this in vain; Glory be to Thee..."[13]

---

[12] Ibid., 190..
[13] āl-'Imrān: 190-1.

Conclusion

Islam is not merely a faith, a 'religion', a creed. It is a way of life - a life to be lived. It does not only respond to man's religious yearnings, but to human life as a whole. It does not only give us an infallible metaphysics, but also a comprehensive and sublime code of individual and social ethics, a sound economic system, a just political ideology - and many other facets of life. It is not a solitary star, but a whole solar system, encompassing the whole and illuminating the whole.

It should be evident, therefore, that the foregoing very brief discussion of a few Islamic aspects is only an introduction to the study of Islam. It is meant to stimulate thought, to bring out the fundamental distinction of Islam from non-Islam, and to show that the notion of religion in Islam is infinitely richer and more sound than any other to which humanity subscribes.

Chapter II

Islam: A Guide

Religion of Humanity and Unity of Allah

Islam teaches the purest form of monotheism (*tawhid*) and regards polytheism (*shirk*) as the deadliest sin. A Muslim addresses ALLAH by His personal Name: ALLAH — the word "God" and its equivalents in other languages being unsuitable in the matter of connotation. Allah, according to Islam, is the One Allah, Who is indivisible in person and Who has no partner, wife, son or daughter. He is the matchless and "nothing is as His likeness". "He begets not, nor was He begotten".[1] He is the First, the Last, the Eternal, the Infinite, the Almighty, the Omniscient, the Omnipresent. He is the Creator, the Nourisher, the Cherisher of all things. He is the All-Just, the Avenger of the wrongs done to the weak and the oppressed, the Compassionate, the Merciful, the Loving, the Guide, the Friend, the Magnificent, the Glorious, the Beautiful and the True. In short, He is the Possessor of all excellence.[2]

Speaking of the conception of Allah in Islam, Gibbon the famous Western historian, says:

> The creed of Muhammad is free from the suspicion of ambiguity and the Qur'ān is a glorious testimony to the unity of Allah. The Prophet of Makkah rejected the worship of idols and men, of stars and planets, on the rational principle that whatever is corruptible must decay and perish; that whatever is born must die, that whatever rises must set. In the Author of the universe his rational enthusiasm confessed and adored an infinite and eternal being, without form or place, without issue or similitude, present to our secret

---

[1] al-Ikhlās: 3.

[2] The *Asmā al-Husnā* (Beautiful Names) encapsulate the attributes of Allah. Refer to surah al-Hashr: 24 which Daryabadi describes as the excellent names.

thoughts, existing by the necessity of his own nature, and deriving from Himself all moral and intellectual perfections. These sublime truths are defined with metaphysical precision by the interpreters of the Qur'ān.[3]

Unity of the Universe

From the unity of the Creator, according to Islam, proceeds the unity of the universe, i.e., unity of Creation and unity of purpose. In other words, the cosmos is a moral order.

Unity of Mankind

Islam regards the whole of mankind as an "organic unity"- a single family, and emphatically says that the distinctions of race, colour, language or territory cannot form the ground for claims of superiority of one group over the other. The only distinction that has value is that of *taqwā* (piety and righteousness).[4]

In a similar vein, Prof. H.A.R. Gibb, the famous English critic of Islam says:

> Islam possesses a magnificent tradition of inter-racial understanding and co- operation. No other society has such a record of success in uniting in an equality of status, of opportunity and of endeavour for so many and so various races of mankind. If ever the opposition of the great societies of the East and the West is to be replacedby co-operation, the mediation of Islam is an indispensable condition.[5]

---

[3] Edward Gibbon, *A History of the Decline and Fall of The Roman Empire* (London, 1881).

[4] Daryabadi's comment on the *āyah* is illustrative of Islam's vision of *taqwā:* "Here indeed is a re-classification of humanity in a promulgation of a new order of nobility – a division of mankind not between princes and peasants, nor between touchables and untouchables but between the more moral and less moral." Daryabadi, *The Glorious Qur'ān* (Leicester, The Islamic Foundations, 2008), 994.

[5] H.A.R. Gibb, *Whither Islam* (London, 1932), 379. Also cited in Fazlur Rahman Ansari,

Unity of Religion

According to Islam, the human intellect, though a great and powerful asset, has its natural limits, and, therefore, neither the normative nor the empirical sciences are capable of leading humanity to an exact knowledge of ultimate truths and the code of life based upon them. The only source of sure knowledge open to humanity is, consequently, divine guidance, and that course has been actually open ever since the beginnings of human life on earth. Allah raised His Prophets and Messengers and revealed His guidance to them for transmission to humanity. Coming from the same source, all revealed religions have, therefore, been one, i.e., Islam .

Allah's Prophets and Messengers continued to come to every country and community to work in their respective limited fields. Time after time, the revealed guidance was either lost or corrupted through human interpolation, and new Prophets with fresh dispensations were sent, and humanity continued to advance from infancy to maturity. At last, when the stage of maturity was reached – when humanity was practically to become one family – instead of sectional guidance, a perfect, final and abiding revelation (*wahy*),[6] addressed to entire mankind and for all time, was granted in the seventh century of the Christian era. That revelation, which recapitulates all former revelations and thus sets a seal on the unity of religion, is Islam; the scripture which enshrines it is the Holy Qur'ān; and the Prophet who brought it is the leader of humanity, Muhammad (pbuh).

Thus all the Prophets of Allah, from Adam down to Noah, Abraham, Moses and Jesus (peace be on them all), are the Prophets of a Muslim, the Holy Prophet Muhammad (pbuh) being the last and final one. All the divine scriptures are the scriptures of a Muslim, though he follows only the Holy Qur'ān because it alone exists in its

---

Islam and Christianity in the Modern World (Karachi,1965), 194.
[6] The nature and function of wahy is elaborated in Ansari's *The Qur'ānic Foundations and Structure of Muslim Society,* vol. I, 51-66.

original purity and it alone contains the religion of Islam which has been followed by all rightly-guided people since the day the first human being came into existence.

Unity of Sexes

Differentiation of functions has misled certain cultures of the world to regard woman as a being who belongs to a different and inferior species and to mete out to her inhuman treatment is therefore just. Islam unambiguously repudiates this notion and teaches that both man and woman have sprung from the same essence and the same source, and consequently possess the same human status. Their functions and interest, instead of being antagonistic, are meant to be complementary. The natural relation between the sexes, in all its aspects, is therefore, that of love and harmony, without which no true human progress can be possible.[7]

Unity of Classes

Islam aims at the creation of a classless society by eliminating all possible social conflicts through resolving the different interests.

In the sphere of economics, Islam lays down the principle that wealth should not be allowed to circulate among the wealthy only, and envisages, through its laws and institutions, a co-operative commonwealth of talents.

In the political sphere, Islam stands for the co-operative commonwealth of the pursuers of righteousness.[8] Taken as a whole, the Islamic state is a welfare state where sovereignty belongs to Allah alone and no human being has a right to govern other human beings except in the name of Allah and according to His Will, and where nobody, not even the head of the State, is above the law. Absolute justice is the watchword and the establishment of

---

[7] Refer to Ansari's lecture *Women in Islam* which analyses the malaise affecting Western society. Yasien Mohamed, *Islam to the Modern Mind,* (Paarl, 2006), 211-26.
[8] The moral and spiritual values as envisaged by Islam can only eradicate economic maladjustment and political manipulation. See Ansari, *Islam versus Marxism,* (Athlone, n.d.) 12-3.

righteousness is the goal.

The merits of Islam's social ethics have elicited praise even from the otherwise hostile critics. H. G. Wells says:

> Islam created a society more free from widespread cruelty and social oppression than any society that had ever been in the world before.[9]

H. A. R. Gibb says:

> Within the Western world Islam still maintains the balance between exaggerated opposites. Opposed equally to the anarchy of European nationalism and the regimentation of Russian communism, it has not yet succumbed to that obsession with the economic side of life which is characteristic of present-day Europe and present-day Russia alike.[10]

Unity of Human Activity

Islam conceives of the human personality as a unity and consequently regards the distinction of secular and religious as unscientific, irrational and absurd. The life of a Muslim, both in its individual and social manifestations, is a life lived for Allah and Allah alone.[11]

"Islam," says Dudley Wright, scholar of comparative religion, "is no mere creed; it is a life to be lived. In the Qur'ān may be found directions for what are sometimes termed the minor details of daily life, but which are not minor when it is considered that life has to be lived for Allah. The Muslim lives for Allah alone. The aim of the Muslim is to become Allah-bound, and to endeavour to advance the knowledge of Allah in all his undertakings. From the

---

[9] H. G. Wells, *Outline of History* (New York, 1921), 325.

[10] Gibb, *Whither Islam,* 378.

[11] The dynamic orthodoxy vision advanced by Ansari is an integrated expression of the human personality. See Abdul Kader Choughley, *Fazlur Rahman Ansari: Life and Thought* (Springs, 2012), 136-8 Cf. Ansari, *Qur'ānc Foundations* vol. I, 157-72.

cradle to the grave the true Muslim lives for Allah and Allah alone."[12]

Religion of "Submission to the Divine Will"

The word Islam means "submission" and, as a religious term, it connotes "submission to the Divine will and commands". As such, Islam is co-extensive with nature. For, everything in nature submits to the Divine will without demur. The only exception is man. He has to choose Islam through his free will and thus to attain his destiny by falling in line with the rest of Allah's creation.

Goethe, the renowned poet-philosopher of Germany, says:

"Naerrisch, dass jeder in Seinem Falle
Seine besondere Meinung priest! Wenn Islam Gott ergeben heisst,
Im Islam leben und sterben wir alle."

It is lack of understanding that everyone praises his own special opinion; (for) Islam means submission to Allah and in Islam we all live and die.[13]

Religion of Nature

The above statement brings out, and the Holy Qur'ān emphasises in clear terms, that to be a Muslim is to live and grow in accordance with true human nature and in harmony with the nature around. Islam, thus, means conformity to the natural law.

---

[12] Dudley Wright, *Prayer* (London, Nicholas Hays, 1981).

[13] Ansari admired the writings of Goethe (d. 1832) which were promoted to a large extent by the poet of the East, Muhammad Iqbal (d. 1938). Many studies have been undertaken to illustrate the affinity of ideas in spirituality and romanticism between Goethe and Iqbal. See Syed Abdul Vahid *Studies in Iqbal,* (Lahore, 1976), 49-78).

Religion of Discipline

The concepts of submission to the Divine will and conformity to the natural law, when actively realised in human life, give rise to the healthiest form of discipline and Islam is the religion of discipline par excellence.

The German Orientalist, Friedrich Delitzsch, admits that the Muslim shows "[owing] to his religious surrender to the will of Allah an exemplary patience under misfortune and he bears up under disastrous accidents with an admirable strength of mind."[14]

Religion of Truth

The concept of truth forms the keynote of Islamic ideology and pervades the entire universal order presented by Islam. Truthfulness is a fundamental value in the elaborate Islamic moral code – a value which forms the foundation-stone of Muslim character. Allah Himself has been mentioned in the Holy Qur'ān as the Truth, or the True, the Holy Prophet Muhammad (pbuh) as the bearer of truth, the Qur'ān itself as the truth, and the abode of the righteous after death as the seat of truth. The following verses (*āyāt*) are reflective of the concept of truth:

$$\text{إِنَّآ أَرْسَلْنَاكَ بِٱلْحَقِّ بَشِيرًا وَنَذِيرًا ﴿١١٩﴾}$$

"We have sent you with the Truth as bearer of glad tidings and a warner."(2:119)[15]

$$\text{ذَٰلِكَ بِأَنَّ ٱللَّهَ نَزَّلَ ٱلْكِتَٰبَ بِٱلْحَقِّ ﴿١٧٦﴾}$$

"This shall be because Allah has surely sent down the Book with Truth.")[16]

---

14 Friedrich Delitzch, *Die Welt des Islam* (Leiden, 1951), 280.
15 al-Baqarah: 119.
16 al-Baqarah: 176.

Religion of Temperance

Islam is the religion of purity and temperance. It stresses purity not only of the mind and the heart, which certain other religions also stress, but also of the body, its fundamental principle being the harmonious development of the human personality. Consequently, it strictly prohibits the use of all drinks and foods which might be unhealthy and injurious to the body, or the mind or both. Thus its prohibitive injunctions cover not only all the intoxicants, e.g., wine, opium, etc., but also those foods which are harmful to healthy human growth. Ultimately, Islamic temperance is the antithesis of evil thoughts, feelings and deeds that stifle the harmonious growth of the human personality.

Religion of Beauty

Unlike certain religions, Islam is not the religion of contempt for the world, or the negation of any fundamental value. It is positively and definitely a religion of fulfilment - fulfilment of all the faculties and positive capabilities with which Allah has endowed man. Aesthetic culture, therefore, is an integral part of Islamic life which of course is governed and controlled by Islam's moral and spiritual principles. In Islam the concept of beauty permeates the entire human activity, in fact, the whole cosmic order. Allah, says the Holy Prophet Muhammad (pbuh), "is beautiful and loves what is beautiful."[17]

Beauty in thought, word and deed, and beauty in all creative activity is the Islamic ideal.

Islam permits the creation of art, within the limitations of its spiritual and moral framework. But its motto is not "Art for the sake of Art" but "Art for the sake of life," whereby a true blending of spiritual, moral, and physical beauty is achieved.

---

[17] Sahīh Muslim, The Book of Faith 1, Chapter 39, Hadith 171.

Religion of Reason

Islam regards reason as man's distinctive privilege and Allah's noble gift. The Holy Qur'ān has repeatedly exhorted mankind to employ reason in matters of social and natural phenomena and in understanding its message and practising its guidance.

Intellectual culture in general, encapsulates one of the noblest pursuits of human life in Islam and the acquisition and cultivation of knowledge has been made obligatory upon every Muslim man and woman.

Religion of the Negation of Superstition

Islam is a positively rational religion and stands opposed to cults and religions of mysterious dogmas whose acceptance is generally claimed on the basis of blind faith.

Speaking of the negation of superstition and the affirmation of reason in Islam, Godfrey Higgins says:

> No relic, no image, no picture disgrace his (Muhammad's) religion. The adoration of one Allah, without mother, or mystery, or pretended miracle, and the acknowledgement that he (Muhammad), a man, was sent to preach the duty of offering adoration to the Creator alone, constituted the simple doctrinal part of the religion of the unitarian of Arabia.[18]

Religion of Action

Islam stands in sharp contrast with those religions which interpret the salvation of man in terms of the acceptance of certain intricate and inexplicable formulae. Simplicity is its watchword and rationality its lifeblood, and as such it gives to both faith and action their due place. Wherever the Holy Qur'ān

---

[18] Godfrey Higgins, *An Apology for the Life of and Character of the Celebrated Prophet of Arabia called Mohamed* (London, 1829).

mentions the problem of human salvation, it points out to right belief (*imān*) as well as righteous action (*a'māl al-sālihāt*)[19], emphasising the former as the basis and the latter as the sequence.

Religion of Balanced Progress

Islamic life is a life of the attainment of *falāh* which means "the furrowing out of latent faculties"[20]. A Muslim, therefore, has to continuously strive for progress, a progress controlled by righteousness and illumined by divine guidance; a progress grounded in spirituality; a progress balanced and comprehending all aspects of human life: spiritual, mental, moral, aesthetic and physical. Paying tribute to the balanced character of Islam and the progress which it inspires, the famous Orientalist,
H. A. R. Gibb says:

> For the fullest development of its cultural life, particularly of its spiritual life, Europe cannot do without the forces and capacities which lie within Islamic society.[21]

Religion of Scientific Quest

While other religions may feel shy of science, Islam has made the scientific quest a religious obligation. The aims of that quest, however, are not the unbalanced indulgence in physical pleasures and the tyrannisation over fellow-beings, but the advancement in the love of Allah through progress in the knowledge of His works and the service of humanity through the acquisition of control over

---

[19] The Qur'ān is replete with verses (*āyāt*) which re-affirm the inseparable link between belief and righteous action. Cf. Surah al-Asr: 3 which provides sequential importance to the concept of salvation.
[20] Ansari states that the term *falāh* has two connotations: actualisation of latent forces, and in sufi parlance, the spiritual development of the latent capabilities that relate to the transcendental dimension of the personality. Ansari, *The Qur'ānic Foundations*, vol. 1, 120, 153.
[21] Gibb, *Whither Islam*, 378.

the forces of nature.[22]

Speaking of the role of Islam as the inaugurator of the modern scientific era, Briffault, the reputed scholar of the history of civilisation, says:

> Although there is not a single aspect of European growth in which the decisive influence of Islamic culture is not traceable, nowhere is it so clear and momentous as in the genesis of that power which constitutes the permanent distinctive force of the modern world and the supreme source of its victory— natural science and the scientific spirit. The debt of our science to that of the Arabs does not consist in startling discoveries of revolutionary theories; science owes a great deal more to Arab culture, it owes its existence.[23]

It is claimed that the Renaissance of Europe owes everything to the revival of Greek thought. H. G Wells, another great Western authority, had to admit that:

> Through the Arabs it was, and not by the Latin route, that the modern world received that gift of light and power (i.e., the scientific method).[24]

Because of its deep-rooted hostility to Islam implanted during the Middle Ages, the West has been very slow in acknowledging the merits of Islam. Admissions and confessions have, however, been gradually coming forth grudgingly or ungrudgingly. Thus, as we have seen above, it has been admitted that the Muslims gave to the West the scientific method as well as the scientific inspiration. But the Muslims themselves received them directly from the Holy

---

[22]See Ansari, Prophet Muhammad's Contribution to Knowledge, in *Moral and Sprititual Transformation in Islam (Springs, 2019)*. Cf. Choughley, *Fazlur Rahman Ansari*, 244-5.

[23] Robert Briffault, *Making of Humanity* (London, 1919), 190.

[24] H. G. Wells, *Outline of History*, 273.

Qur'ān. This fact has also been admitted at last.

Challenging the adversaries of Islam and referring to the Holy Qur'an, Dr. A. Bertherand says:

> Let them read and meditate on this great Book: they will find in it, at every passage, a constant attack on idolatry and materialism; they will read that the Prophet incessantly called the attention and the meditation of his people to the splendid marvels, to the mysterious phenomena of creation... those who have followed its counsels have been the creators of a civilisation which are astounding to this day.[25]

Religion of the Sanctity of Labour

In Islam, all honest labour is sacred and forms the lifeblood of human progress. The Holy Qur'ān says:

$$وَأَن لَّيْسَ لِلْإِنسَٰنِ إِلَّا مَا سَعَىٰ ﴿٣٩﴾$$

"For man is naught but what he strives for..."[26]

"The labourer is the beloved of Allah," says the Holy Prophet Muhammad (pbuh). Thus idleness is a vice and industry is a virtue in Islam.

Religion of the Highest Idealism in Ethics

Islam lays the foundation of ethics on "submission to the Divine Will" and gives to humanity the ethical ideal of imitating the Divine Attributes, even as we have been exhorted by the Holy Prophet Muhammad (pbuh) who says:

"Imbue yourselves with Divine Attributes."

---

[25] *Contribution des Arabs au Progres des Sciences Medicales*, 6.
[26] an-Najm: 39.

Religion of Peace and Goodwill

The word *salām* which means peace, has a close root- affinity with the word Islam. Thus the concept of peace is intrinsically linked to the word Islam itself. Indeed, this concept permeates the Islamic religion through and through. For, Allah, according to the Holy Qur'an, is As- Salām, i.e., the (source of) peace. A Muslim's salutation, which embodies the ideal of Muslim life, is *As-salām-u-'alaikum,* i.e.'Peace be unto you'; and the abode of the righteous, towards which the Holy Qur'an invites humanity, is *dār-al-salām,* i.e. "the abode of peace."

One of the ideals of Muslim life therefore, is the attainment of peace on all fronts – peace with self through harmonious self-realisation, peace with fellow-creatures through the maintenance of the basic attitude of goodwill, and peace with Allah through submission to the Divine Will.[27]

Religion of Struggle (*Jihād*)

The Islamic concept of peace is not, however, utopian. For, Islam is a practical religion —a religion of struggle (*jihād*)— and does not, therefore, prescribe any course of action which is unnatural or impracticable. Thus, for instance, in international relations, although basically committed to the promotion of peace and goodwill, Islam does allow the participation of Muslims in war when it becomes morally inevitable—when no other course remains open for safeguarding justice or peace itself.

Jihād which has been much maligned refers to struggle which according to Islam is of two kinds:

- Struggle for subjugating one's lower self to the higher self. This is the higher form of *jihād* and its function   is purely

---

[27] For a detailed discussion on the concept of peace, see Ansari, *The Qur'ānic Foundations,* vol. I, 368-2.

spiritual;
- Struggle for defeating the forces of evil on the collective plane. This is the collective *jihād*.

The collective *jihād* may, again, be either of a peaceful character, namely, propagation of Islam and its establishment in the collective life of the people through preaching and reform, or it may be in the form of war against an aggressor.

The Islamic permission of war, is by and large, for defensive purposes. And not only does Islam rule out all immoral impulses to war but it also lays down a ideal code of ethics which in its sublimity and humaneness surpasses all other ethics of war which humanity has ever known.

"In their wars of conquest," says E. Alexander Powell, "the Muslims exhibited a degree of toleration which put many Christian nations to shame."[28]

Religion of No Compulsion in Conversion

As regards forcible proselytisation, it has been explicitly banned by Islam with the Qur'ānic declaration:

"There is no compulsion in matters of faith..." (2:256)[29]

The propaganda that Muslims went out into the world with the sword in one hand and the Qur'ān in the other to convert the non-Muslims forcibly is a pure fabrication. Indeed, it is so utterly unfounded that even an enemy of Islam like Rev. Dr. O'Leary had to admit:

History makes it clear that the legend of fanatical Muslims sweeping through the world and forcing Islam at the point of sword

---

[28] E. Alexander Powell, *The Struggle for Power in Moslem Asia* (New York, 1923), 48.
[29] al-Baqarah: 256.

upon conquered races, is one of the most absurd myths that the historians have ever repeated.[30]

Religion of Brotherhood

Islam inculcates the love of Allah's creation in general and of the human family, in particular.

"The best of you is he who is the best to Allah's family (i.e., humanity)," says the Prophet (pbuh).

Islam regards humanity as one fraternity through which it affirms the existence of the Islamic brotherhood. Hence all distinctions of caste and tribe, race and colour, language and territory, are superseded and obliterated.

Side by side with the code of conduct meant to be observed within the circle of Islamic brotherhood, Islam also gives a definite code of ethics which relates to the interaction of Muslims within the larger human society.

The Dutch orientalist, Snouck Hurgronje observes:

> The ideal of a league of human races has been approached by Islam more nearly than by any other ideology: The League of Nations founded on Muhammad's religion, which takes the principle of the equality of all human races so seriously as to put other communities to shame.[31]

Religion of Spiritual Democracy

In the sphere of worship, Islam stands for the establishment of a direct relation between Allah and man without the mediation of any priest.

It is wrong to regard the scholars (*'ulama*) or the leaders (*imāms*) of congregational prayers in the mosques as priests. Any good Muslim who knows Islam can lead the prayers, while the *'ulama*

---

[30] Muhammad Asad has succinctly analysed the myths of the Crusade mentality against Islam in his *Islam at the Crossroads* (Lahore, 1969), 62- 82.
[31] Snouck Hurgronje, *Muslim World Today* (London, 1967). Cf. S.S. Leeder, *Veiled Mysteries of Egypt* (London, 1912),332-5.

are scholars and experts of Islamic knowledge and merely fulfil a responsibility which rests on the shoulders of the entire Islamic brotherhood. Islam wants every Muslim man and woman to be a scholar of its teachings, unlike, for instance, Hinduism, where those belonging to the caste of Brahmins alone posses this privilege.

Rev. W. Wilson Cash, the famous Christian missionary and hostile critic of Islam, had to confess:

> Islam endowed its people with a dignity peculiarly of its own. Direct access to Allah makes one of the strong appeals of Islam.[32]

Religion of Human Dignity

Problem of Slavery

By declaring freedom as the birthright of all human beings and by proclaiming human equality, Islam states that the progeny of Adam is the noblest creation of Allah. It raised humanity to the status of the vicegerency of Allah on earth, by making imitation of the Divine Attributes the ethical ideal of mankind, and by pointing out to the conquest of the universe as the human destiny. In short, Islam has established human dignity on the loftiest pinnacle conceivable.

Humanity was suffering in various ways because of the wrong notions held by pre-Islamic cultures and religions about human dignity, when Islam appeared. Cruelty was being perpetrated in the name of caste, tribe and race. Large masses of humanity had been reduced to the status of serfs, and slavery which had been an age-old institution, was being practised by various races and peoples of Europe and Asia, including the Arabs. Islam promoted a philosophy and a legislation which has made it the saviour of the down-trodden and the oppressed for all time.

Among the many misconceptions spread about Islam by its enemies, one is that which relates to slavery. For a proper

---

[32] Wilson Cash, *The Expansion of Islam* (London, 1928).

appreciation of the role of Islam in the abolition of slavery, the reader is referred to the present writer's *Islam and Slavery*.[33] We confine ourselves to the brief statement of the Dutch critic of Islam, Suouck Hurgronje who said:

According to the Muhammadan (Islamic) principle, slavery is an institution destined to disappear.

Religion of Rational Sexual Morality

Problem of Polygamy

The Islamic view of the fundamental equality of sexes has been already stated in the section on *Religion of Unity* and an impartial historical appreciation of the problem proves beyond all doubt that it was "Islam which removed the bondage in which women were held from the very dawn of human history and gave them a social standing and legal rights such as were not granted to them in England till many centuries later."[34] But the widespread propaganda of the enemies of Islam in connection with polygamy necessitates a specific statement in this regard.

In the first instance, polygamy was not invented by Islam, nor was it made in any way obligatory. It had existed in pre-Islamic societies since times immemorial with the sanction of religion and had been practised even by those who were accepted as holy personages as, for instance, in the Old Testament. There it was governed by no law whatsoever, and so also was it in the Arabian society at the advent of Islam. What Islam did was to regulate it and to subject it to such severe restrictions as to make it prohibitive except in cases of emergency. Indeed, monogamy has been the ideal and polygamy only an exception in Muslim society. This fact is fully borne out by the present as well as the past history of the Muslims and has been admitted by all fair-minded critics of Islam.

Islam is a natural religion and it takes a very serious view of sexual

---

[33] Ansari, *Islam and Slavery* (Karachi, WFIM).
[34] Lady Cobbold, *Pilgrimage to Mecca* (London, 1910).

vices and social ills. Consequently, it was very natural for Islam to permit limited and restricted polygamy for the maintenance of social health in all those situations where it is the only natural remedy. For instance, when war alters the natural sex ratio, giving to women a preponderance over men, there are only two alternatives, namely, widespread prostitution or polygamy. Islam prefers the latter to the former in the interest of moral health and social well-being of womanhood. Similarly, if the first wife is sterile or suffers from any incurable disease, there are only two possible alternatives, namely, either the first wife should be divorced and a second wife taken or she may continue in her status undisturbed along with a second wife. The former course would mean distressing spinsterhood for the first wife while the latter course would provide her with an honourable normal life without temptation to evil.

Polygamy can also become a necessity in a medically incurable case of the hypersexed male who, in most cases, would look to more than one woman for the satisfaction of his biological need. In all such cases, the Islamic permission of polygamy with all its responsibilities and restrictions would be a definitely healthier course than the hypocritical adherence to the formal monogamy.

Polyandry (i.e., the marriage of one woman with several husbands) is not permitted in Islam because psychologically it is unsound, sociologically it is impracticable, and biologically it is most dangerous for the physical health of the persons concerned. Certain primitive tribes who practise polyandry are infested with the plague of venereal diseases.

Speaking on polygamy, Dr. Annie Besant says:

> There is pretended monogamy in the West, but there is really polygamy without responsibility; the 'mistress' is cast off when the man is weary of her and sinks gradually to be the 'woman of the street', for the first lover has no responsibility for her future, and she is a hundred times worse off than the sheltered wife and mother in the polygamous home. When we see thousands of miserable women who crowd the streets of Western towns during the night, we must surely feel that it does not lie in Western mouth to reproach Islam for

polygamy. It is better for a woman, happier for a woman, more respectable for a woman, to live in polygamy, united to one man only, with the legitimate child in her arms, and surrounded with respect, than to be seduced, cast out into the streets, perhaps with an illegitimate child outside the pale of law, unsheltered and uncared for, to become the victim of any passer-by night after night, rendered incapable of motherhood, despised of all.[35]

Religion of Salvation in this Life and the Hereafter

It is the distinctive merit of Islam that it does not concern itself merely with salvation beyond the grave but also gives full consideration to human salvation in this   life. For that purpose, it provides comprehensive guidance which guarantees moral perfection, social progress, economic justice and political stability—in short, all that   is needed for the practical realisation and attainment of true happiness in earthly life and all-round harmonious evolution of humanity.

Religion with Authentic and Perfect Divine Scripture

There are three fundamental merits of the Holy Qur'ān, the scripture of Islam, in which it stands unique among the scriptures of the world. They are:

- authenticity of its text;
- perfection of its literary form;
- rational character, comprehensiveness and profoundness of its guidance.

Even a brief discussion of these merits is not possible in the present introductory sketch. They are, however, so well-established that even the non-Muslim Western scholars, who are always ready to

---

[35] Annie Besant, *The Life and Teachings of Muhammad* (Madras, 1932), 25- 7.

attack Islam on the slightest pretext have had to admit them in forceful words.

Commenting on the beauty of form of the Holy Qur'ān, Paul Casanova remarks:

> Whenever Muhammad was asked a miracle as a proof of the authenticity of his mission, he quoted the composition of the Qur'ān and its incomparable excellence as a proof of its divine origin. And, in fact, even for those who are non-Muslims nothing is more marvellous than its language: its simple audition ravished with admiration those primitive peoples so fond of eloquence! The ampleness of its syllables with a grandiose cadence and with a remarkably large rhythm have been of much moment in the conversion of the most hostile and the most sceptic.[36]

As regards perfection in matter of guidance and the authenticity of its text, Laura Veccia Vaglieri observes:

> But besides the perfection of form and method, the Book is also inimitable by its very substance, for, we read in it, among other things, provisions of future events, and of references to accomplishments since many centuries or which are generally ignored, and allusions to the most different sciences, religious or profane. On the whole, we find in it a collection of wisdom which can be adopted by the most intelligent of men, the greatest of philosophers and the most skilful politicians. But there is another proof of the divinity of the Qur'ān: it is the fact that it has been preserved intact through the ages since the time of its Revelation till the present day. And so it will always remain, with Allah's Will, as long as the universe exists. Read and re-read throughout the Muslim world, this Book does not rouse in the faithful any weariness; it rather, through repetition, is more and more loved every day. It gives rise

---

[36] *L' Enseignement de l'Arabe au College de France, Lecon d'Ouvenrture*, April 26, 1969.

to a profound feeling of awe and respect in the one who reads it or listens to it.[37]

Religion with the Simplest Creed

The Islamic creed is as simple as much as its ideology is profound. Its fundaments are:

Six Articles of Faith

They are: Belief in: (1) Allah; (2) Angels; (3) Divine Scriptures; (4) Messengers of Allah; (5) the Hereafter; (6) the pre-measurement of good and evil.

The "Five Pillars"

They are:

1. Declaration of faith in the oneness of Allah and in the divine Messengership of Muhammad (pbuh)
2. Prayers (*salāh*)
3. Obligatory Fast(*sawm*)
4. *Zakāh* or Poor-tax
5. Pilgrimage to the Ka'bah at Makkah by those who possess the means (*hajj*).[38]

A Christian critic of Islam makes the following confession:
Islam had the power of peacefully conquering the souls by the simplicity of its theology, the clearness of its dogma and principles, and the definite number of practices which it demands. In contrast to Christianity which has been undergoing continuous transformation since its origin, Islam has remained identical with itself.

---

[37] *Apologie de L'Islamisme*, 57-9.
[38] For a fuller appreciation on the articles of faith and principles of Islam, see Abdul Aleem Siddiqui, *The Principles of Islam* (Karachi, 2002).

Here it may be noted, however, that these six articles and five pillars constitute only the first "fundamentals" and that which is enshrined in the Holy Qur'ān and the sunnah are so comprehensive as to cover the entire sweep of necessary guidance on physical, moral, social and spiritual aspects of human life.

Muhammad: The Pinnacle of Human Perfection

A code alone cannot, by its existence as such, inspire mankind to action. Hence to love the Holy Prophet Muhammad (pbuh) above all human beings and things of the world, to believe in him as the most perfect embodiment of human perfection and as the absolute leader and the last and the final Prophet (after whom no new prophet of any categoryis to come)[39] and to follow him as the best example, form the prerequisite of Islamic belief.

This is the theological status of the Holy Prophet Muhammad (pbuh) in Islam. As regards his refulgent personality, that would require volumes even to do justice to it.

It is said that "the best testimony is that which comes from the enemy's camp." Here, therefore, we might quote a few statements of the Western scholars of Islam.

The Holy Prophet (pbuh) was an embodiment of humility. The following account reveals his extraordinary personality.

"Muhammad's figure was highly majestic, his complexion and features were extremely handsome, and "he was gifted", says the renowned Orientalist Lane Poole, "with mighty powers of imagination, elevation of mind, delicacy and refinement of feeling. 'He is more modest than a virgin behind her curtain', it was said of him. He was very affectionate towards his family. One of his boys died on his breast in the smoky house of the nurse, a blacksmith's wife. He was very fond of children; he would stop them in the

---

[39] Here Ansari makes reference to Qadianism which sought to give religious credibility to its founder, Ghulam Ahmad Qadiyani, who claimed peculiar forms of prophethood. See Mohammed Elias Barney, *Qadiani Movement* (Durban, 1955).

streets and pat their little heads. He never struck anyone in his life. The worst expression he ever made use of in conversation was, 'What has come to him? May his forehead be darkened with mud!"

"When asked to curse someone, he replied, 'I have not been sent to curse but to be a mercy to mankind.' He visited the sick, followed any bier he met, accepted the invitation of a slave to dinner and mended his own clothes.

"He was the most faithful protector of those he protected, the sweetest and most agreeable in conversation. Those who pbuh him were suddenly filled with reverence; those who came near him loved him; those who described him would say, 'I have never seen his like either before or after."

"He lived with his wives in a row of humble cottages separated from one another by palm branches cemented together with mud. He would kindle the fire, sweep the floor, and milk the goats himself. The little food he had was always shared with those who dropped in to partake of it. Indeed, outside the Prophet's house was a bench or a gallery on which were always found a number of poor who lived entirely upon his generosity, and were hence called 'people of the bench'. His ordinary food was dates and water, or barley bread; milk and honey were luxuries of which he was fond but which he rarely allowed himself."[40]

Speaking of the glorious success which attended the Holy Prophet Muhammad's mission, Carlyle observes:

To the Arab nation Islam was a birth from darkness into light; Arabia first became alive by means of it. A poor shepherd people, roaming unnoticed in its deserts since the creation of the world; a hero- Prophet was sent down to them with a word they could believe: see the unnoticed becomes world-notable, the small has grown world-great. Within one century afterwards, Arabia is at Granada on this

---

[40] Stanley Lane-Poole, *Speeches and Table Talk of Prophet Muhammad* (London, n.d), 28-30.

hand, at Delhi on that, glancing in valour and splendour and the light of genius, Arabia, shines through long ages over a great section of the world. These Arabs, the man Muhammad, and that one century— is it not as if a spark had fallen, one spark on what seemed black, unnoticeable sand? But lo! the sand proves explosive powder and blazes heaven-high from Delhi to Granada! [41]

O. Houdas, the French scholar, said half a century ago about the inner vitality of the Holy Prophet's message:

> Never has a religion developed with parallel rapidity. In less than half a century Islam spread from the banks of the Indus to the shores of the Atlantic Ocean, and, if this movement slowed down, it still persists after thirteen (*fourteen*) centuries of existence. After having penetrated in India, in China and Malaya, Islam continues its invading march in the African continent which will before long become entirely Muslim. Without special missionaries and without resort to the force of arms, the religion of Muhammad has converted the Black continent, and it is not without some astonishment to point out the existence in England and America of small white communities which have adopted the Islamic doctrines and made efforts to propagate them. This invasion of Europe, hardly visible today, will surely grow.[42]

Absorption in the Love of Allah: The Final Goal

Cultivation of and absorption in the love of Allah, and the permeation of the heart with the sweet ecstasy of that love, until a person becomes virtually incapable of acting against the Divine commands, is the final goal, which bestows upon a Muslim

---

[41] Thomas Carlyle, *Heroes and Hero Worhsip* (London, 1888).
[42] Le Grande Encyclopaedie, *Tome 20 Islamisme.*

abiding life—a life of peace, progress and perfection.

43

Chapter III

Philosophy of Worship ('*Ibādah*) in Islam

Concept of Worship ('*Ibādah*)

The concept of worship in Islam is unique among the religions of the world. The word which the Holy Qur'ān has used for worship is '*ibādah*, which means submission to Allah and service to Him. The term worship conveys the meaning of adoration in the English language. In Arabic, the word '*ibādah* denotes the act of becoming '*abd*, namely, slave. Consequently, the full connotation of this term refers to an '*abd* who negates himself entirely and affirms the supremacy and absolute authority of Allah in all aspects.

Worship forms only a part of human life in other religions. In Islam it is meant to cover the whole gamut of life. Other religions are dualistic. They divide the world between two water-tight compartments i.e. bearing two different labels of the religious and the secular. For instance, Christianity preaches with all the force at its command: *Give unto Caesar what is Caesar's and unto God what is God's.* Similarly, Hinduism, Judaism, Buddhism and Zoroastrianism teach an irreconcilable conflict between the physical and the spiritual. Hence, the acts of worship in all these religions are purely devotional and ceremonial in the same way as they are in Christianity.

The fact is that all the non-Islamic religions are basically committed to the doctrine of dualism, and consequently they stand for condemning the worldly relations as outside the scope of religious life. Therefore, their notion of worship is of a partial type and is confined to rituals and ceremonies. Islam, on the other hand, refuses to acknowledge dualism and affirms monism or a unitary outlook toward life. It teaches that because Allah is absolutely good, all His actions must always be good, whether they pertain to the domain of the spirit or to the realm of matter. The universe is the act of Allah. It is Allah's creation. Hence it is essentially good.

Believing the world to be essentially evil, the great non-Islamic religions teach escape from the world and the obligations of worldly life as the way to attain saintliness. Islam, on the other hand, teaches the fullest utilisation of physical situations and guiding the social life to its maximum potential.

According to Islam, it is an insult to Allah for man to despise as worthless anything that He has created, and to refuse to bring into play the different faculties and powers with which He has endowed man.

Now, the different faculties which Allah has given to us fall under five categories:

1. Physical
2. Mental
3. Moral
4. Aesthetic
5. Spiritual.

Islam wants us to live a life wherein all these different faculties and the corresponding aspects of human activity are optimally realised. This is so because Islam does not regard the worldly life as evil. It is essentially good and can become evil only if it is pursued for its own sake or in obedience to one's passions and appetites. But if the worldly life is led in obedience to the commands of Allah, every worldly act becomes an act of worship (*'ibādah*).

Side by side with teaching this philosophy of transforming the whole life into one of worship, Islam also outlines the ceremonial acts of worship because they too

play a vital role in building up the human personality. Such ceremonial acts of worship have been given to us in Islam in the form of the following three institutions:

1. Obligatory institutional prayers (*salāh*)
2. Fasting (*sawm*)
3. Pilgrimage (*hajj*)

Zakāh is also included among the *'ibādah* or devotional acts because it entails sacrifice of money at regular periods and according to a fixed rate in submission to the command of Allah. It is, however, distinguished from prayers, fasting and pilgrimage inasmuch as it does not involve any ceremonies. In fact, strictly speaking, there are only two devotional institutions in Islam which involve ceremonies, and they are prayers (*salāh*) and pilgrimage (*hajj*). It may be remarked in passing that the Muslim jurists have also included marriage among ceremonial devotions. We are not, however, concerned with that here.

We may now take up the rationale behind prayers (*salāh*), fasting (*sawm*), *zakāh* and *hajj* (pilgrimage).

Prayer (*Salāh*)

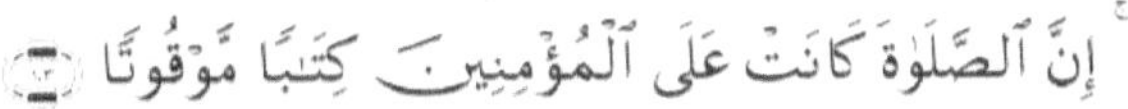

"Verily the prayer is prescribed to believers at definite times..."[1]

Islam has been built up on five Pillars—one of faith and four of action - and prayer (*salāh*) forms the most important pillar of action. The question arises here as to what is the need of Prayer? It is an age-old conviction of humanity that the human personality is constituted of three factors, body, mind and soul. It is also an established fact that it is the nature of human personality to develop and evolve. The law of evolution has been universally acclaimed as the true principle underlying the existence of all organisms. All of us know that the human body is an evolutionary phenomenon. We are told in biology that the earliest form of every human baby that comes into this world is that of a life-germ, which is just an infinitesimal speck and unnoticeable by the human eye. This speck evolves in its embryonic stage by acquiring more and more developed forms, until it develops into a full-fledged human personality and comes into this world to play its role in the life of humanity. We also know that when a human being enters the world, it has all the human features and human

---

[1] al-Nisā: 103.

limbs; but it is not yet fully grown. Rather, its physique has to undergo a continuous process of development day in and day out, for years and years, and then alone it acquires maturity of physique—although even then its physical possibilities are not completely exhausted.

Similar to the physical evolution is the process of the evolution of human consciousness. There are three levels of consciousness-instincts, reason and intuition while there are five forms of consciousness - physical, theoretical, moral, aesthetic and spiritual consciousness.

When a human baby comes into this world, its reason and intuition are dormant. Even all the instincts are not active. In fact, the only instinctive activity present at the time of birth is in connection with the sense of taste. The eyes of the baby open only a day or two after birth, but even then the sense of sight is in a very simple and vague form. For instance, the child does not seem to distinguish between different objects, which capacity develops only gradually. In the same way do all other senses develop.

Thus human reason starts functioning only when the primary senses have developed to an appreciable extent. This occurs when the child has learnt to talk and begins to ask questions. Then begins his education in which he gets the opportunity of developing his intellect. This situation continues for some time when the third stage is reached: the moral consciousness starts asserting itself. It continues to deepen and widen as life progresses. Moral development, in its turn, leads to two further realms, firstly of aesthetic and then of spiritual consciousness.

It must be clear at this stage that it is not only the human body which evolves from a life-germ into a full- fledged state, but the human consciousness also evolves through a continuous process.

Now, the human body cannot develop and evolve without being fed and taken care of. Similarly is the case of human mind and human soul.

We feed the human body with physical food. We feed the human mind with ideas or mental food. Likewise, we must feed the human soul with spiritual food.

There is a whole science of dietics and nutrition concerning the human body. There is a whole system of education for the cultivation of the mental faculties and for feeding the mind. What should be our attitude to the human soul, then? The only rational and natural answer to this question, is that, just as we try to feed the body with different types of food, and just as we try to feed the mind continuously, it is also our duty to feed the soul un-interruptedly.

We have already pointed out that the food for the body is physical in its nature while the food for the mind is mental in its approach. Therefore, the food for the soul should be spiritual. We have been told in Islam that the food for the soul is the remembrance of Allah (*dhikr*). It is to be performed in a state of communion, with similar pre-requisites that we observe in the administration of physical and mental foods.

The first pre-requisite in connection with the physical food is to eat it with preparation and care. Mental food too has to be received with dedication and the fullest attention. Likewise spiritual food must be administered after preparation, which Islam prescribes in the form of pre-prayer ablution (*wudhu*), establishing the intention (*niyyah*) and withdrawing the thought from everything and concentrating it upon Allah. This form of devotion refers to the act of remembering Allah with both heart and soul.

The second pre-requisite in connection with the physical food is that it should be of a healthy type. Likewise, is the situation with mental food: the ideas which can ensure the healthy development of the mind are always those which are sound and good. As regards our spiritual food, our remembrance of Allah should be centred on the One and True Allah and not on man-made deities and idols. Thus Islam has laid the most profound emphasis on the avoidance of polytheism (*shirk*) and believing in the One and Only Allah as alone worthy of worship.

The third pre-requisite in connection with the physical food is that it should be administered at regular intervals during the day and the night; otherwise the physical organism will not grow properly or may not grow at all. A similar regular routine is essential for feeding the mind. Training must be consistent in order to build up the human mind in a healthy state and on a sound pattern. Likewise, the third pre-requisite of feeding the soul should be regular and consistent feeding, and this Islam has provided in the most natural form by prescribing the five obligatory prayers during the day and the night, or, during one cycle of night and day. The Fajr (morning) *salāh* is observed before sunrise when the day is about to begin and we have to plunge ourselves wholeheartedly into our major engagements. It forms the spiritual breakfast and is timed to act as a forerunner of the physical breakfast. Then there comes a lull in our physical stamina at noon when we have to replenish our energy by having lunch. Islam prescribes that we should revitalise on that occasion our spiritual energy also by offering the Zuhr (mid-day) *salāh*. Later in the day we again need a cup of tea or some light refreshment. Islam desires us to have a spiritual stimulant also at that time in the form of 'Asr (afternoon) *salāh*. Again, when the sun sets and the night begins and a new phase starts and the time for dinner comes, Islam wants us to reinforce our spiritual energy also by means of the Maghrib (sunset) *salāh*. Later on comes the time for going to bed when healthy and strong people like to take some nutrient in order to pass the night in radiant sleep. Islam desires us to strengthen ourselves spiritually through the 'Isha (night) *salāh* and to go to bed while we are in a state of spiritual harmony.

Fasting (*Sawm*)

شَهْرُ رَمَضَانَ ٱلَّذِىٓ أُنزِلَ فِيهِ ٱلْقُرْءَانُ هُدًى لِّلنَّاسِ وَبَيِّنَتٍ مِّنَ ٱلْهُدَىٰ وَٱلْفُرْقَانِ ۚ

"The month of Ramadān: in it was sent down the Qur'ān, a guidance to mankind and with evidence..."[2]

We know that the human body needs not only nutrition in the

---

[2] al-Baqarah: 185.

form of food but also medical treatment whenever it loses its balance or any function of the body gets impaired. Similar is the case with the human soul: Islam has taken the greatest care to ensure that it obtains not only the spiritual food but also the appropriate spiritual medicine which has been prescribed in the form of obligatory fasting during the month of Ramadān and optional fasting at other periods during the year.

Although fasting is essentially spiritual medicine, it is also a great remedy for medical defects and ailments, so much so that even the most serious diseases can be cured through certain types of fasting without the aid of medicine.

Reverting to the spiritual aspect of life: the greatest enemies of man are those that reside within his own person as, for instance, greed, lust and passion which pertain to the lower self (*nafs-al-ammārah*).

It is because of these baser appetites that human beings have the overpowering desires to commit crimes of intemperance against the body, the mind and the soul; and they wrong others by committing different types of injustices against them. It is again these baser appetites which cause human beings to deny spiritual values and to forget Allah.

Now, the only way to subjugate the lower self is to constantly perform psychological and spiritual exercises. In this way acts of aggressiveness are brought under control and they start obeying the dictates of reason. He whose life is governed by the baser self is worse than beasts. He whose life is governed by reason is really man. He whose life is governed by spiritual aspirations and enlightenment based on the love of and obedience to the One True Allah, undoubtedly he is pure gold because he rises above the angels in stature. This is the goal which Islam has set for every Muslim and for this purpose Islam has prescribed the obligatory and the optional fasts.

Zakāh

Zakāh is one of the pillars of Islam and, as such, stands next in importance only to institutional prayer (*salāh*). While *salāh* is an obligation towards one's own self and towards Allah, *zakāh* is an obligation towards others. The Holy Prophet Muhammad (pbuh) has laid down the law about *zakāh* saying: "It is to be taken from the rich and given to the poor." This means that *zakāh* is a tax which is levied on those who can save after satisfying their basic needs, and is utilised for those who do not possess the means of fulfilling their basic needs.

Zakāh has been conceived in Islam as a state- institution. It is meant to be collected by the Islamic state and to be deposited in the state bank as a social welfare fund. In Islam, it is the obligation of the state to guarantee the basic needs to all the citizens, which is fulfilled through the institution of *zakāh*, as the Holy Qur'ān says:

$$\text{إِنَّمَا ٱلصَّدَقَٰتُ لِلْفُقَرَآءِ وَٱلْمَسَٰكِينِ وَٱلْعَٰمِلِينَ عَلَيْهَا}$$

$$\text{وَٱلْمُؤَلَّفَةِ قُلُوبُهُمْ وَفِى ٱلرِّقَابِ وَٱلْغَٰرِمِينَ وَفِى سَبِيلِ ٱللَّهِ}$$

$$\text{وَٱبْنِ ٱلسَّبِيلِ ۖ}$$

"Verily, charity is meant for the destitute and those who are short of means, and the officials (of the department of zakāh), and those who are converts and their financial difficulties entitle them for help, and for the emancipation of slaves, and for extricating the people from the burdens of their bad debts, and for the defence of Islam, and for assisting the stranded travellers..." (9:60)[3]

Since some time a social insurance tax has been levied by certain Western governments and it is said that the step is a landmark in

---

[3] al-Tawbah: 60.

the history of social welfare. But it was Islam which instituted the department of social welfare and guaranteed the welfare of all its citizens for the first time in the history of mankind. This department was inaugurated and organised by the Holy Prophet (pbuh) himself and it continued to develop as the Islamic economic order. During the rule of Caliph Umar, it assumed its full-fledged organisational structure. He established the Diwān, i.e. the Bureau of Statistics, wherein the particulars of every citizen were recorded and as a consequence everyone who required help was assisted financially without any hardship and to the fullest extent. Those who were incapable of earning, namely, the elderly people, the crippled, the orphans and the widows were granted pensions and stipends. Those who were capable of earning but were unable to enter into trade because of a lack of financial resources were provided the fullest assistance. The positive results through such sustainable development projects were that within thirty years after the advent of Islam, and more particularly during the rule of Caliph Umar, not a single family could be found who would accept *zakāh*. This meant that every Muslim had become so rich or self-sufficient that he or she was paying *zakāh* rather than being in need of accepting it.

Pilgrimage to Makkah (*Hajj*)

ٱلْحَجُّ أَشْهُرٌ مَّعْلُومَٰتٌ فَمَن فَرَضَ فِيهِنَّ ٱلْحَجَّ فَلَا رَفَثَ وَلَا فُسُوقَ وَلَا جِدَالَ فِى ٱلْحَجِّ ۝

"The season of Hajj is the months known so whoever enjoins upon himself the Hajj therein there is to be no lewdness nor wickedness nor disputing during the Hajj...")[4]

Pilgrimage to Makkah (*hajj*) is one of the five pillars of Islam and enjoys an eminent place among Islamic religious institutions. We

---

[4] al-Baqarah: 197.

might mention here certain spiritual and social benefits which it confers on the pilgrim:

1. A Muslim is a person who is meant to be Allah- conscious in all the actions of his life and this higher consciousness is cultivated in Islam by means of different Islamic institutions like prayers, fasting and *zakāh*. It is in the *hajj*, however, that it assumes its highest form, for the pilgrim is required not only to give up his regular work for a number of days, for the sake of journey to Makkah and the participation in congregational communion with Allah there, but he must in addition, sacrifice many other amenities and comforts of life. Cut off from the worldly pursuits in this manner, he undergoes a spiritual experience of the highest type. Every member of the great assemblage at Makkah sets out from his home with this object in view. He discards all those comforts of life which act as a veil against the inner spiritual experience. He puts on the simplest un-stitched dress and he is required to avoid all indecent thoughts, all evil talks and all disputes. All the prayers and all the symbolisms which he observe during the *hajj* express only one ideal and only one goal: absorption in the love of Allah. It is the same when he runs between the hills of Safā and Marwā and it is the same when, like a moth whirling around a flame, he makes *tawāf* (circumbulation) around the Ka'bah.

2. The *hajj* excels all other institutions of the world in its wonderful influence in leveling all distinctions of race, colour and rank. Not only do people of all races and all countries meet together in the House of Allah as members of one family, but they are all clad in the same dress - the same two sheets of seamless white cloth – and there remains nothing to distinguish the high from the low.